Oh, How He Loves You

Also by Corrie ten Boom

Oh, How He Loves You

Corrie ten Boom

Fleming H. Revell
A Division of Baker Book House Co
Grand Rapids, Michigan 49516

He Cares, He Comforts © 1977 by Corrie ten Boom
He Sets the Captive Free © 1977 by Corrie ten Boom

Published by Fleming H. Revell
a division of Baker Book House Company
P.O. Box 6287, Grand Rapids, MI 49516-6287

Previously published separately as *He Cares, He Comforts* and *He Sets the Captive Free*. Published together in 1985 as *Jesus Is Victor,* which also included *Don't Wrestle, Just Nestle.*

Printed in the United States of America

Library of Congress Cataloging-in-Publication Data

Ten Boom, Corrie.
    [He cares, He comforts]
    Oh, how He loves you / Corrie Ten Boom.
       p. cm.
    Originally published as two works: He cares, He comforts; He sets the captive free, c1977, in series: Jesus is victor.
    ISBN 0-8007-1776-7
    1. Consolation. 2. Ten Boom, Corrie. 3. Christian biography—Netherlands. 4. World War, 1939–1945—Personal narratives, Dutch. 5. Ravensbrück (Concentration camp) 6. Christian life. I. Ten Boom, Corrie. He sets the captive free. II. Title.
    BV4905.2.T46 2000
    269'.2'092—dc21   00-03661
    [B]

Unless otherwise indicated, Scripture quotations are from the King James Version of the Bible.

Scripture quotations identified LB are from *The Living Bible* © 1971. Used by permission of Tyndale House Publishers, Inc., Wheaton, IL 60189. All rights reserved.

Scripture quotations identified NIV are from the HOLY BIBLE, NEW INTERNATIONAL VERSION®. NIV®. Copyright © 1973 by International Bible Society. Used by permission of Zondervan Publishing House. All rights reserved.

Scripture quotations identified PHILLIPS are from *Letters to Young Churches* by J. B. Phillips. Copyright © 1947, 1957 by Macmillan Publishing Co., Inc., renewed 1975 by J. B. Phillips. Used by permission.

Scripture quotations identified RSV are from the Revised Standard Version of the Bible, copyright 1946, 1952, 1971 by the Division of Christian Education of the National Council of the Churches of Christ in the USA. Used by permission.

For current information about all releases from Baker Book House, visit our web site:

http://www.bakerbooks.com

Contents

Publisher's Preface

Corrie ten Boom was an unforgettable woman—unforgettable not only because of her bravery in hiding Jews during the Nazi occupation of Holland, not only for her courage in the concentration camps, but also in her later years for the way she gained instant and genuine rapport with her worldwide audiences and for the comfort and care she exuded in her constant stream of correspondence.

This book in the Corrie ten Boom Library series combines two smaller books previously published as *He Cares, He Comforts* and *He Sets the Captive Free*.

Part 1, "He Cares, He Comforts," deals with the difficult subjects of pain, abandonment, bereavement, and shame. Corrie tells how she met many people in her travels who were understandably dejected and depressed because of what they had experienced. Then she tells how God gave each of them comfort and assurance, allowing

them to rejoice in the midst of their afflic-
tion. We hope these pages will help you do
the same.

In part 2, "He Sets the Captive Free," Corrie states that many people are captives just
as much as she was in Nazi Germany. Some
people are caught in circumstances from
which they cannot extricate themselves.
Others are enslaved by habits or problems
of the past or difficult home situations. Corrie's message in this section is one of freedom and forgiveness found in God's love.
Here she shares some of the secrets that
sustained her in prisons and concentration
camps. These same principles will also help
you as you strive to obtain victory over those
things that hold you in captivity.

In *Oh, How He Loves You,* you will find
not only the assurance of God's love for you
but also the freedom He offers those who
follow Him.

Dear Friend

Through my travels around the world and through my books and films, I have made many friends. When they are ill, I should love to be able to visit and comfort each of them. But I do pray for them, and the Lord gave me this idea—to write them a letter!

That was the beginning of this book. I prayed that the Lord would guide me and give me the thoughts, remembering what I had experienced with sick friends, and He gave me one after the other.

Often friends have the same problems, the same kind of suffering, and that's why I wrote down all I could remember. I think one of these stories I tell may have an answer for you, from Corrie, but given to Corrie by the Lord. So in some way it is a greeting, a message from the Lord Himself, who loves you and has your life in His hands, who knows of every suffering, every problem, as no human being does.

I also want to share with you what I learned during my imprisonment. I want to share my experiences with you to show you that even when circumstances look utterly bleak, there is a victorious life that is real and available to you.

It is not only behind barbed wire or prison doors that there are prisoners. There are prisoners of sin, of lust, of wrong philosophies, of circumstances, of self. I pray that this book will help you to lose your life for Jesus' sake so that you may gain it. Jesus said that those whom He makes free are free indeed.

If you do not know Him, this book will be a challenge, an invitation from the Lord, who said, "Come unto me, all ye that . . . are heavy laden, and I will give you rest" (Matt. 11:28). If you know Him already, it will be a message from that Friend you and I have in Jesus.

Oh, how He loves you!

PART 1

He Cares,
He Comforts

1

That Wee Little Baby

Yesterday I met a lady who is expecting a baby. I always like to pray with such a mother and to pray for the baby she has under her heart.

"Lord Jesus, You love that baby already. You know it and You can already fill that tiny little heart with Your love. Lord, will You give the baby and the mother strength and health for the time of pregnancy? And also for the birth? Bless the doctors and the nurses and give them wisdom and love." I was happy that I could pray with that mother, for I know that the Lord hears our prayers.

Some time after that, I was lying in the sunshine and I think I had fallen asleep, for I had a dream. I was talking with that wee baby for whom I had prayed! Often in dreams things happen that cannot take place in reality, for that little baby was talking with me too!

"I am very happy to be here in this very safe corner of the world. It is so warm and so quiet here under Mama's heart. I have enough food and I do not at all long to be born! I am sure life must be difficult and noisy! No, I want to stay here always."

In my dream, I answered, "No, you must not think about being born as something that is sad or wrong. It is a joy to be born, for then life, the *real* life, begins. You will see your mother's face and her eyes full of love for you. You will rest in her arms, and you will feel her arms around you. Then you will grow up and become a strong person. After you have lived for a time, there will come a moment when you have to go through another birth: when you go from this world to heaven. It will be like the time when you came from the little place under your mother's heart into life. Then you will see the eyes of Jesus and you will rest in His arms and He will bring you to a beautiful house that He has been preparing for all who believe in Him."

I awoke, and I had to laugh. But I was also happy about that dream. It was good. I took the Living Bible and read, "You made all the delicate, inner parts of my body, and knit them together in my mother's womb. . . . You saw me before I was born" (Ps. 139:13, 16 LB).

Are you afraid to die? Remember that for a child of God, death is only a passing through to a wonderful new world—to the house with many mansions where Jesus has prepared a place for you.

> For we know that when this tent we live in now is taken down—when we die and leave these bodies—we will have wonderful new bodies in heaven, homes that will be ours forevermore, made for us by God himself, and not by humans hands.
>
> 2 Corinthians 5:1 LB

If you don't have that assurance, please read on. I will tell you more about how to be ready.

2

The Little Lamb

---- ·〰〰· ----

It is always a tragic thing when a child dies. People have a tendency to call this an injustice on the part of God. However, God owes us nothing. If He gives our child ten years and then takes him away, we must be grateful for those ten years.

Also, I know how the Lord can use such happenings to accomplish a good purpose. I once heard about a mother who lost her child. She was very embittered and rebellious. One day she walked alone in the fields with a heavy heart. Suddenly she noticed a flock of sheep. The shepherd was trying to make the sheep cross over a narrow bridge into another field, but the sheep did not want to set their feet on the shaky little bridge. They went right and left and turned just like stupid sheep do, but they did not obey the shepherd. Finally, the shepherd grabbed a little lamb that had been pressing itself against the soft wool of its mother's body. The man now carried the little lamb across the narrow bridge and put it into the meadow on the other side. Immediately, the mother sheep, bleating loudly, followed across the bridge, and then all the others followed.

The bereaved mother had observed all this with interest. Suddenly she knew that this was a message for her. She realized that for many years she had stubbornly gone her own way instead of following the call of the Good Shepherd: "Come unto me!" Now He had taken away her little son and brought him safely to the other side. His purpose was that she would come to Him and lead the way for many others to be saved. This is what happened. She went to the Lord and gave Him her heart and life. Then she was able to be a witness to many others and help them to find the way to the Good Shepherd.

3
A Happy Visit

She was the mother of one of my club girls and had asked me to visit her in the hospital. When I arrived, she was lying in a bed in a big ward, and she was looking very happy.

"I am really having the time of my life," she said. "Never have I had such good care. I do not have to cook—they bring my meals to my bed—and the nurses even wash me. My, that is different—quite different—from being at home and taking care of my naughty boys."

I understood what she meant. She lived in a narrow alley and had a rather rough husband and many children. "Oh," she said, "it is such a joy that the nurses look after me in every way! I like being ill."

"I understand, but tell me, are you in pain?"

"Yes," she said, "I still have pain, but I must tell you more about why I am so happy. The woman next to me told me more about Jesus. My daughter, who is in your club, also told me about Him, but here I really had time to think. She gave me a tract and a small Bible. I have been reading them and feel so happy! She read Psalm 23 to me and I understood that the Lord *is* my Good Shepherd. Isn't that wonderful? There is only one almost insurmountable obstacle, and that is that next week I must go home again. I feel happy, but I also feel rather weak. I lost so much blood, and I do not feel strong. Then to have to go back and start everyday life again."

I understood and said to her, "Listen, you know now that the Lord is your Shepherd and takes care of His sheep. When you are at home, the same Jesus, who now gives you peace in your heart, will be your Guide and your Friend. What a Friend we have in Jesus! He will help you with all the work you have to do at home. He helped you here! When I was a little girl, five years old, I asked Jesus to come into my heart, and He became my best friend. Now that was a long time ago, but I know He never lets you down. At home, you will find that He is your teammate. Do you have difficulties and problems?"

"Yes, I have many. Big boys are not easy these days."

I could tell her that every person in the world is very important in God's eyes and that Jesus, when He died on the cross, bore our sins and sorrows and our punishment. If she would go to Him, He would in no wise cast her out. I prayed with her, and then I heard her whisper, "Jesus, I did not know You, but I would like to be the sheep that You find and take into Your arms. Will You also forgive me my sins? Amen."

I was happy about that and again I saw that there is nobody in the world who can say, "I cannot come to Jesus, He will not accept me."

Come unto me, all.

Matthew 11:28

He loves you and is very happy if you say, "Yes, Jesus, I want to belong to You."

For God so loved the world, that he gave his only begotten Son, that whosoever believeth in him should not perish, but have everlasting life.

John 3:16

4

Pain

———— ✺✺✺ ————

I visited Bob, a friend who had had a terrible accident. When I entered his room, he opened his eyes and looked at me, saying only one word: "Pain." I saw on his face that his suffering was almost unbearable. I stayed with him that evening.

There came a moment when I saw that he was able to listen, and I told him an experience I had in the concentration camp. "Bob, the greatest suffering I had in the concentration camp was to be stripped of all my clothing and to have to stand naked. I told my sister, 'I cannot bear this. This is worse than all other cruelties we have had to endure.' Suddenly it was as if I saw Jesus on the cross, and I remembered that it says in the Bible, 'They took His garments.' Jesus hung there naked. By my own suffering, I understood a fraction of Jesus' suffering, and that gave me strength. Now I could bear my

own suffering. Love so amazing—so divine—
demands my life, my soul, my all. Bob, do
you realize it must have meant almost intol-
erable pain for Jesus to die on the cross? Just
think of His hands, His feet, His body. And
He did that for you and for me."

I was silent. Bob had closed his eyes. But
a moment later he looked at me and said, "I
am looking at Jesus. Yes, I understand only a
fraction of the pain He suffered. And it makes
me so thankful that He did it all for me."

Bob's face was more relaxed than before,
and I saw peace in his eyes. A moment later
I saw that he had fallen asleep, and I qui-
etly left the room.

The next day I was able to visit him again.
"Corrie," he said, "every time I had so much
pain and could hardly bear it, I was thinking of Jesus. It made me so thankful! It is as
if now I have the strength to bear it. Tell me
a little bit of what you thought when you
had to suffer in the concentration camp.
Have you ever had pain?"

"I surely have, and do you know what
helped me then?

> The sufferings of this present time are not
> worthy to be compared with the glory which
> shall be revealed in us.
>
> Romans 8:18

"We can look forward to the time when we shall be in the place where there is no pain, no cruelty, no death. Oh, Bob, the best is yet to be! Isn't that a joy?"

I saw him smiling for the first time. "Yes," he said, "what a joy! The best is yet to be!"

> And God shall wipe away all tears from their eyes; and there shall be no more death, neither sorrow, nor crying, neither shall there be any more pain: for the former things are passed away.
>
> Revelation 21:4

5

Can You Forgive?

———————— ❧❧❧ ————————

One day I visited an old friend in a hospital. When I entered her room, I saw that she was very ill, but also that there was an expression of bitterness on her face. We had many things to talk about, for we had not seen each other for a long time. Then she told me about her husband.

"I know that I will be ill for a long time. The doctor does not give me any hope that I can do my work for a long time to come. My husband did not like having a sick wife. He left me and now lives with a younger woman. He never comes to see me."

"Have you forgiven him?"

"No, I certainly have not!"

"I will tell you something of my own experiences, when I felt bitter about someone. It was in Germany. One day I saw a lady in a meeting who did not look into my eyes. Suddenly I recognized her. She was a nurse

26

who had been very cruel to my dying sister when we were in Ravensbrück concentration camp during the war. When I saw her, a feeling of bitterness, almost hatred, came into my heart. How my dying sister had suffered because of her! The moment I felt that hatred in my heart, I knew that I myself had no forgiveness. It was the Lord Jesus who said to us, 'If ye forgive not men their trespasses, neither will your Father forgive your trespasses' (Matt. 6:15).

"I knew I had to forgive her, but I could not. Then I had a good talk with the Lord about it when I was at home later. 'Lord, you know I cannot forgive her. My sister suffered too much because of her cruelties. I know, Lord, that I must forgive, but I cannot.' Then the Lord gave me, 'The love of God is shed abroad in our hearts by the Holy Spirit which is given unto us' (Rom. 5:5).

"The Lord taught me a prayer: 'Thank You, Lord, for Romans 5:5. Thank You, Jesus, that You brought into my heart God's love by the Holy Spirit who is given to me. Thank You, Father, that Your love in me is stronger than my hatred and bitterness.' The same moment I knew I could forgive.

"I told a friend about my experience and she said, 'Oh, I know that nurse. She works in a hospital not far from here.'

"'Can you call her?'

"'Sure I can.' She called the nurse, and I had a talk with her over the telephone, telling her that when I had the next meeting that evening, I would have a different message and would very much like her to come.

"Her answer was, 'You would like to see *me* in your meeting?'

"'Yes, that is why I phoned. I should like it very much.'

"'Then I will come.' She did come, and during the entire evening she looked into my eyes while I spoke. After the meeting, I had a talk with her. I told her that I had been bitter, but that God's Holy Spirit in me had brought His love instead of hatred and that now I loved her. I told her that it was through Jesus Christ who bore our sins on the cross. He forgave us, but He also fills our hearts with God's love through the Holy Spirit, and that is why I could invite her to come to the second meeting.

"I told her more, and at the end of our talk that nurse accepted the Lord Jesus Christ as her personal Savior and Lord. Do you see the miracle? I, who had hated her, was used by God to bring her to the acceptance of Jesus Christ. Not only will the Lord cleanse us by His blood, but He will also use us. He used me, who hated her, and God had so absolutely forgiven and cleansed *me* that He could use me to show *her* the way of salvation!

"You are bitter about your husband, but claim Romans 5:5. I know that you love the Lord Jesus. You have known Him for a long time. Trust Him to do the miracle of bringing into your heart so much of God's love that you can forgive your husband!" I prayed with her and left.

A week later I was once more in her room. When I saw her, I knew that God had done something in her heart. "I am absolutely free. The Lord has done in me such a tremendous miracle that I could forgive my husband. You know, now there is a great peace and joy in me."

Yes, we never touch the ocean of God's love so much as when we love our enemies. It is a joy to *accept* forgiveness, but it is almost a greater joy to *give* forgiveness.

The love of God is shed abroad in our hearts by the Holy Spirit which is given unto us.

Romans 5:5

6

The Foolishness of God

━━━━━ ✖✖✖ ━━━━━

After World War II, my friends and I organized a former concentration camp in Germany as a shelter for the homeless. Once, when I went there, I found a man (a lawyer) who was seriously ill. I asked him if he knew the Lord Jesus. "No," he said, "as long as I do not understand things with my brains, I cannot believe them."

I had a talk with him, and I told him that in 1 Corinthians, chapters 1 and 2 tell us about the wisdom of the wise and the foolishness of God. "In the Bible," I said, "you can read very much about the foolishness of God. It is the highest wisdom. It is more important than the wisdom of the wise, because it is only through this that you get the real vision."

It was some weeks later that once more I was in our camp, and I went straight to my friend. He was even more ill than the first time I had seen him. I asked, "What do you think of the foolishness of God?"

"I can praise the Lord, for I have seen that it is the greatest wisdom. I have thrown away my pride, and I have come to Jesus as a sinner and asked forgiveness. I thank Him for His death on the cross, and I can tell you that He has brought into my heart a peace that passes all understanding. It surpasses everything of the wisdom of the wise, but it is the greatest reality I have ever experienced in my life. I am so thankful for the Bible. During these weeks I have read much in it, and I do not fear the future, whatever happens."

> Neither death, nor life, nor angels, nor principalities, nor powers, nor things present, nor things to come, nor height, nor depth, nor any other creature, shall be able to separate us from the love of God, which is in Christ Jesus our Lord.
>
> Romans 8:38–39

For the first time I saw him look really happy!

> Hath not God made foolish the wisdom of this world? . . . Because the foolishness of God is wiser than men; and the weakness of God is stronger than men.
>
> 1 Corinthians 1:20, 25

7
Alice

※※※

In the concentration camp, a girl once came to me and said, "Please, will you come to Alice a moment? She has such terrible nights. While we sleep, she always turns from one side to the other. She suffers. I don't know what it is. Can you help her?"

"Sure," I said, "I can help her. I can pray for her. But I am busy here with a group. We are studying a portion of the Bible. In a quarter of an hour I will come to Alice."

When I went to her, I saw that she had fallen asleep. She was very restless, tossing from one side to the other. I spoke softly to her, but she did not hear me. Then I prayed and said, "Lord Jesus, You can fill Alice's heart with Your peace. You can fill her subconscious with Your love, and then she will sleep well."

As I said amen to that prayer, I saw that Alice was quiet. She slept, and I knew that the Lord had answered my prayer.

The next morning, my friend who had called me the day before said, "Oh, Corrie, it was a joy that Alice slept so well. She was so quiet—and I know that God has answered your prayer."

That day Alice died, but I had enjoyed an experience that has given me much courage. When we pray, every word we say is heard by the Lord, and I even read in the Book of Revelation that our prayers are kept in heaven. Our intercession is so important!

Often we cannot reach the others, but the Lord can reach everyone. What a joy to have such a Savior!

Pray one for another.
James 5:16

8
Tommy

He was one of a big family. I believe there were fourteen children. Tommy was at a special school for mentally handicapped persons. I gave Bible lessons in that school.

Sometimes I visited Tommy in his home. When I asked where he was, his mother always said, "He's in his room upstairs." I knew where to find him—in the little corner of the attic that was his "room." It was nothing more than a bed and a chair. On the chair there was always a small picture of Jesus on the cross.

I remember that once when I visited him, Tommy was on his knees before that chair. His face was full of joy. "Tommy, why are you so happy?" I asked.

"Because Jesus loves me!" he said. "And I love Jesus. He died on the cross for me and my sins, and now I have forgiveness."

His mother told me that Tommy always went straight to his little room when he came home. It was quiet there—a corner of peace in the rather small house. With so many children, the house was often noisy.

One day she found him with his head on the chair. In his hand was the picture of Jesus. Tommy did not move. He was with the Lord.

I'm sure that when he died, he must have felt great joy, because Jesus loved him and had died for him on the cross—and he knew it! Do you know it too? Jesus, who loved Tommy, loves you just as much.

> For God so loved the world, that he gave his only begotten Son, that whosoever believeth in him should not perish, but have everlasting life.
>
> John 3:16

9
Toontje

─────────── ❧ ───────────

In Haarlem, my hometown, there was a minister who told me of a little boy who was feebleminded. His name was Toontje. He was always sitting in the front pew of the church. The minister said to his wife, "Toontje doesn't understand one word of my sermons. Nevertheless, he is so faithful—he comes every Sunday."

Once the pastor spoke of the ocean of God's love and told how we knew of it through Jesus Christ. When he was talking, he saw on Toontje's face an expression of great joy. Toontje understood when he talked about God's love. I myself worked among the feebleminded, and I know from experience that you can never speak too much about the love of God.

The next day the pastor went to Toontje's home. He thought he would see if the boy still knew something of God's love. But when he arrived at Toontje's house, he heard that the boy had died in his sleep. The pastor told me that on Toontje's dead face was an expression of heavenly joy. "I believe," he said, "that Toontje tried to get too much of God's love into his heart, so that his heart just broke for joy."

If you and I would also accept too much of God's love, our hearts could break for joy. But in heaven we shall have such strong hearts that they will contain much, much more of the love of God. Oh, what a joy that will be! Then we shall praise and thank Him for all He was and is and shall be for us. Hallelujah! What a Savior!

We can only see a little of the ocean
    when we stand at the rocky shore,
But out there, beyond the eye's horizon,
    there's more—there's more!

We can only see a little of God's loving,
    a few rich samples of His mighty store,
But out there, beyond the eye's horizon,
    there is more—there is more!

                                    Author Unknown

We can read in the Bible:

As I think of this great plan I fall on my knees before the Father (from whom all

fatherhood, earthly or heavenly, derives its
name), and I pray that out of the glorious
richness of his resources he will enable you
to know the strength of the Spirit's inner
re-inforcement—that Christ may actually
live in your hearts by your faith. And I pray
that you, rooted and founded in love yourselves, may be able to grasp (with all Christians) how wide and long and deep and
high is the love of Christ—and to know for
yourselves that love so far above our understanding. So will you be filled through all
your being with God himself! Now to him
who by his power within us is able to do
infinitely more than we ever dare to ask or
imagine—to him be glory in the Church
and in Christ Jesus for ever and ever, amen!

Ephesians 3:14–21 PHILLIPS

10
Mother

I would like to tell you a little bit about my mother. I loved her so very much. The last years of her life she was very ill, and she could not even talk well—only a few words. But she could love, and she could receive love. It was before she fell ill that we had a talk about the Lord.

Mother said, "I am not quite sure if everything is all right between the Lord and me. My faith is so little."

I told her words of Jesus, such as, "Come unto me, all." I said, "Mother, you, too, belong to the *all*."

Mother looked sad and answered, "Yes, but . . ." These words so often interfere when the Lord speaks to us, if we listen more to the spirit of doubt than to the Lord.

And now Mother was ill. She had had a stroke and could say only a few words. One day I brought her a breakfast tray. She folded her hands and then shook her head. I asked, "Mother, can you not even find words when you pray?"

"No." But then she looked at me, and I saw that her face was relaxed and happy.

"But it does not matter that you cannot talk to the Lord," I said. "He talks to you, doesn't He?"

"Yes," she said, and her face was beaming with joy.

"Is it all right with you and the Lord?"

"Absolutely!" was her reply.

I tried to find out the reason she was so changed from doubt to trust. "Did we say something, Mother? Or did someone else who visited you, perhaps the pastor who came to see you yesterday? Or was it a message over the radio that gave you the assurance of salvation?"

Mother smiled and then she pointed upward with her finger.

"Was it the Lord who made it all right?"

"Yes, absolutely, it was the Lord." Six words Mother said, and what a joyful sentence!

My! There I saw that even when we could not reach her, the Lord could always reach her. And He is more concerned about our well-being than we are for each other. When

I told Father, he said, "Oh, this is an answer to my prayer!"

"Did you also pray for it? I did too." We found out that the whole family had been praying that the Lord might give Mother great assurance instead of doubt. How He had answered that prayer! What a joy it was!

Later on, Mother grew worse and was very, very ill; then she could not talk at all. It was as if she had no consciousness, but I felt her pulse, and then I talked and asked her some questions. Her heartbeat went quicker when I spoke. "Mother, when you are going to die, you have nothing to fear, for you know that Jesus died on the cross for the sins of the whole world, and also for your sins. And, Mother, He is preparing a beautiful house for you in heaven. Then you may go there, and we shall see each other again. For the Lord loves us and we all love Him! Just think of it, Mother, in heaven we shall have no pain. There will be no sickness at all, and, Mother, there you will see Jesus. What a joy it will be to look at His wonderful face!"

I knew that although she could not speak at all, she had understood what I had said. But do you understand what made me happiest? To know that when we cannot reach the other one, the Lord can reach His beloved. And it is He who has said, "Lo, I am with you alway, even unto the end of the world" (Matt. 28:20).

I know that He was with Mother when she died and went home. He Himself brought her into His wonderful paradise. "Promoted to Glory," the Salvation Army people say.

> Thou has beset me behind and before, and laid thine hand upon me.
>
> Psalm 139:5

11
Pietje

Pietje was a hunchback. She was one of my club girls. We liked each other and had a lot of fun. She could neither walk very far nor very fast, and I also had difficulty keeping pace with the other girls of my club. I remember we were on a trip one time through Germany, and we had to cross a rather high mountain. Pietje came to me and said, "Auntie, give me your hand and I will help you." We both had to laugh, for she understood that I needed her help and she needed mine, so we stayed a little behind the rest of my healthy club girls and went arm-in-arm up the mountain.

Yes, Pietje was a dear girl. I remember that in the youth hostel where we stayed that evening, we had a talk about the judgment day of God. Pietje said, "I'm afraid to come before the judgment seat. Have we any advocate who will plead for us?"

"Well, just look in the Bible."

Christ . . . maketh intercession for us.
Romans 8:34

"That is good!" Pietje said. "Who is our judge?"
"Read it yourself."

Who is he that condemneth? It is Christ.
Romans 8:34

"What? Jesus Christ is our Judge *and* our Advocate? Now I am not afraid anymore! He will plead us not guilty."

That girl was so happy because she saw what a joy it is that Jesus died for us on the cross and carried our punishment. She knew that one day He will be our Judge and our Advocate. Yes, that was a good talk we had together, there in that youth hostel! I remember there was a lovely view over the mountains and the sun was setting with beautiful colors.

Later, I had to visit Pietje when she was very ill. I found her in the corner of a huge ward in a big hospital. When I saw her, there was nobody with her—no visitors and no nurse—and I talked with her.

"Will you stay with me until I die?" she asked.

"Yes," I said, "I'll do that. Are you sure that you will die soon?"

"Yes," Pietje smiled. "I'm not at all afraid, for, you know, my Judge is the Advocate and my Advocate is the Judge. I am not afraid at all, because it is Jesus Himself who loves me and I love Him."

Say, do *you* sometimes fear when you think of the judgment day of God, where we all have to appear whether we believe it or not? Read your Bible! Jesus is *your* Judge and *your* Advocate. Isn't that good? We have nothing to fear—*nothing!*

Who is he that condemneth? It is Christ that died, yea rather, that is risen again, who is even at the right hand of God, who also maketh intercession for us.

Romans 8:34

12
Debbie

———— ❧❧❧ ————

A friend of mine told me about her sister Debbie. She was very ill and needed some comfort. "I know," my friend said, "that you cannot go all the way to Missouri to visit her, and she cannot come to you. But what about having a talk over the telephone?" That was a good idea. Isn't it wonderful to live in a world where we can talk with each other over the telephone?

It was a good conversation. She told me her difficulties and her worries. "Corrie," she said, "I'm very ill, and some people think I must die. I am afraid of death. Can you help me?"

"Yes, surely, but listen. We haven't much time to talk over the telephone, so let us just ask each other some questions and give answers. Do you know the Lord Jesus? I don't ask if you know *about* Him, but do you *know* Him?"

"I'm not sure. I have not read much in the Bible. I did not go to church and was really not greatly interested in spiritual things, so I feel that I do not really know Jesus."

"Then first of all you must come to Him, for He is the One who can comfort and help you. He said, 'Come unto me, all ye that labour and are heavy laden, and I will give you rest' (Matt. 11:28). 'Him that cometh to me I will in no wise cast out' (John 6:37).

"And when you come to Him, He is willing to come so close that He will even come into your heart. 'Behold, I stand at the door, and knock: if any man hear my voice, and open the door, I will come in' (Rev. 3:20).

"Do you understand that *you* must open the door? Then He will come in and you can tell Him everything. He understands far more than I—or any other human being—can. It is true that when you come into contact with the Lord Jesus, you will see your sins, but look at the cross then. You must simply say, 'Lord Jesus, forgive me. I thank You that You died on the cross for my sins.' The Bible says that then He will cast your sins into the depths of the sea, forgiven and forgotten. And I believe that He adds a sign that reads NO FISHING ALLOWED! What about that?"

"I will think about it."

"No, listen! It is all right to think about it, but we have so little time now. Why not do it?"

"Do what?"

"Ask Jesus to come into your heart!"

"Is it so simple?"

"Yes, so simple!"

Then I prayed with her. Oh, it is such a joy that we can always pray with one another over the telephone—the line to the Lord is never busy. He is always ready to listen. "Lord, Debbie would like to ask You to come in, and I thank You, Lord, that You are willing. Will You send away all the doubt, all the 'yes, buts' and the 'if onlys'? I thank You, Lord, that You love Debbie. Hallelujah! Amen!

"Now, Debbie, the way is open. Say, 'Come into my heart, Lord Jesus.'"

And she did. I heard her say, "Lord Jesus, come into my heart. I know that I am not good enough, but, oh, Lord, how I need You! Thank You, Jesus, that You came into my heart. I will tell You all the sins I can remember, and I thank You that You have borne them on the cross. Oh, Lord Jesus, You love me. Thank You. And I love You. Amen."

Now, wasn't that a wonderful prayer? I was so happy, and I know the Lord was happy. I could imagine Him standing there with His arms wide open. I said also, "Debbie, now tell Him all your fears and problems and be sure that when you feel very ill, the Lord Jesus is with you. He will not let you down for one moment."

"Are you sure?"

"Yes, for I know the Lord. I have known Him for a long time, and He never gives in. And you two will win, Jesus and you. Bye, Debbie. Until we meet, not in Missouri, but there—in heaven."

"Thank you, Corrie."

I was so happy about that telephone call. But I could do something more for her, and that was to pray! And I did: "Lord, make her very conscious of Your presence. And, Lord, surround her with Your angels and let her room be a room where she is together with You and the angels."

Some time afterward, I met her sister again, and she said, "Oh, Corrie, very shortly after you had spoken with Debbie, she became more ill and I went to her to be with her until the end. She repeated all you had said over the telephone. 'I did it,' Debbie told me. 'I didn't understand everything but I know that He came, for since that time there has been such peace and joy, and there is no fear at all. I know that I have to die soon, but do you know that I long to go to be with the Lord in heaven?'"

What a blessed telephone talk that was!

> Jesus did it,
> The Bible tells it,
> I believe it.
> That settles it!

Come unto me, all ye that labour and are heavy laden, and I will give you rest.

Matthew 11:28

13
Passing the Baton

─────── ✖ ───────

You know that I am a *Tramp for the Lord*. I traveled all over the world to tell others about the Lord Jesus. I am already old and I do not like to go alone. That is why I always have a younger woman with me. At one time, the Lord gave me Connie to accompany me. For more than seven years, we went together over a large part of the world. But she married, and then the Lord gave me another companion.

There came a time when Connie became very ill, and she knew that she had to die.

Her husband came home one evening and saw that she was crying. He put his arm around her and asked, "Connie, why do you cry?"

She answered, "I traveled much with Tante Corrie and after that I traveled much with you. But now I must go on a journey all alone and you and Tante Corrie will not be with me."

"Oh, but listen, Connie," said her husband. "I will keep your hand in mine, and in the moment when you really die, I will give your hand into the hand of Jesus. He will keep you through the valley of the shadow of death and bring you to the beautiful heaven where He has prepared a house for you!"

Connie did not cry anymore. What her husband had said was so true! And it all happened that way when Connie went home.

Oh, that loving hand of God! The men who wrote the psalms knew much when they wrote what the Holy Spirit told them, "If I take the wings of the morning, and dwell in the uttermost parts of the sea; even there shall thy hand lead me, and thy right hand shall hold me" (Ps. 139:9–10). "Thou art my strength. Into thine hand I commit my spirit" (Ps. 31:4–5).

Connie had a husband who was with her until the last moment of her life. Many, many people have no husband who is able and has the opportunity to stay with them when they are dying, but the great joy is that everyone can know there is a Savior in Jesus Christ. "What a Friend we have in Jesus!"

His hand keeps us, not only when we go through the valley of the shadow of death but also before that. When we pray, "Take my hand, Lord, and hold me tight," the Lord does it. He has every opportunity and every possibility—and how much love He has for us! He is never too busy with others. He takes time to be with us. He Himself said, "Lo, I am with you alway, even unto the end of the world" (Matt. 28:20).

My father used to say to us, when we were children and had to go away from home for a while, "Children, don't forget, when Jesus takes your hand, then He holds you tight. And when Jesus keeps you tight, He guides you through life. And when Jesus guides you through life, one day He brings you safely home."

14

Used by God

———————— ✂️ ————————

Once I slept in a hospital in a concentration camp. Many people were ill and many died. In the night, I heard people calling, and I went to them. I was ill myself, but not so seriously that I couldn't do this—I went to everyone who called. I saw much, much suffering and loneliness there.

It was in that concentration camp hospital that I experienced God's use of sick people to help others around them. You can feel so weak in illness and unable to do anything, but witnessing for the Lord Jesus is possible because it is really the Lord who witnesses *in us* and it causes us to relax. When we are channels of living water, then it is the Lord who tells us what to say, and He *never* makes a mistake.

Nobody was with these dying people, but I could tell all of them, "Jesus is here. Just put your hand in His hand." And many of them did. Then I saw peace coming into the hearts of these people. There is a little poem in Holland:

> *Als wij de doodsvallei betreen,*
> *laat ons elke aardse vriend alleen,*
> *maar, Hij, de beste Vriend in nood,*
> *geleid ons over graf en dood.*

When we enter the valley of the shadow
   of death,
all our earthly friends leave us alone,
but He, the best Friend in need,
accompanies us through the grave and
   death.

Yes, even for people who are surrounded by friends and relatives, a moment comes when they have to turn to Jesus—the only One who can help them. But what a joy that He is there!

I saw a nurse who looked so worried and tired. Every time she passed my bed, a woman next to me smiled to her, and sometimes she said a kind word.

In the evening the nurse came to her and said, "Do you know that you have helped me? My day was full of disappointments, but your smile has encouraged me."

I learned an important lesson that evening.

15
Nobody Is Too Bad

⁓⁓⁓

During the war in Vietnam, I was permitted to visit a hospital. I talked to the men who were wounded. In a ward with about twelve patients, I had an opportunity to speak. I told them about the living Jesus, who is with us, who loved us so much that He died for us, and who now lives for us. He is at the same time at the right hand of the Father, praying for us. I also told them that He said, "Come unto me, all ye that labour and are heavy laden, and I will give you rest" (Matt. 11:28). I showed them what a joy it was that we could come to Him.

Afterward, I had a talk with the man sitting next to me. He was not much more than a boy and seriously wounded. He said to me, "What you told about Jesus is so beautiful, so joyful! But I cannot do what you said and go to Him. I have heard about the Lord, but I have always blasphemed.

When there were boys in my class who followed the Lord, I teased them. There has
been hatred in my heart—hatred against
God—and now I know that I am seriously
wounded. But I have been too bad; I cannot go to the Lord. I am ashamed of what I
have done, of how I have tried to keep others away from Him. Now don't tell me that
I can ask Him to help me. I am a very wicked
fellow."

"There is only one kind of person who
cannot come to Jesus," I told him. "They are
the ones who think and say, 'I'm so good, I
don't need forgiveness, I don't need the Savior.' They are the Pharisees, and you can
read in the Bible that Jesus could not and
would not help the people who were so
proud of themselves and who thought they
were so good.

"You are quite different. You think you are
too bad. You are not. Jesus bore the sins of
the whole world, and that is a lot. He has
also borne your sins on the cross: sins of
hatred, of blasphemy, of whatever you did.
You *can* go to Him. Jesus hates sins but loves
sinners, and all His promises are really for
sinners only. *You* are not good enough; *you*
are not able. It is *Jesus* who is able, and He
is your Savior. Just talk to Him! Tell Him

what you have done and what you have been, and then ask forgiveness. The Bible says that when you bring your sins to Him, He will blot them out like a cloud. Did you see that cloud this morning? It is gone. It will never come again. It has absolutely disappeared forever. So when you bring your sins to Jesus, He will make them disappear—He will destroy them forever and ever."

Suddenly I saw that all the men in the ward were listening. I asked, "Who of you will now come to Jesus as a sinner? When you know you are a sinner, you are forgiven." Many men in that ward responded.

> If we confess our sins, he is faithful and just to forgive us our sins, and to cleanse us from all unrighteousness.
>
> 1 John 1:9

16
Niwanda

I saw a little paper in my hand. I don't know who put it there, but it was a letter: "Please, come to me. I am in the fifth bed at the right. Niwanda."

I was in Africa and had spoken that morning in a boys' boarding school. I asked the missionary if he could help me find out from whom that letter had come. He smiled and said, "Yes, I know. That boy is very ill. We could not yet take him to the hospital. Fifth bed, that is in room three. I can take you there."

We entered the room where we found Niwanda. Immediately I saw that he was really ill. "I needed some help to find you!"

We both laughed, and the missionary said, "I will leave you alone with him."

Niwanda and I had a good talk together. "Tell me something of yourself."

"I am very ill. I have been a Christian for a long time and I have served God, but when I look back on my life, I feel so ashamed. I read in the Bible that Paul said, 'I have fought a good fight.' When I look at the past, I know that I, too, have really done my best to fight the good fight. But no, I didn't make a good job of it as Paul did."

"Listen, Niwanda. It is true that Paul wrote, 'I have fought the fight.' We can quite agree because we have such great respect for him. But he did not write, 'I have fought the fight the right way.' He means, 'I have been fighting in the good fight.' You and I also have to do so—we are both in the good fight. We stand on victory ground, because our fight is under King Jesus, and King Jesus is Victor. He makes us more than conquerors."

I saw that the boy looked happy when I told him about fighting while standing on victory ground.

I have fought a good fight, I have finished my course, I have kept the faith.

2 Timothy 4:7

17
His Sheep

———— ✦ ————

Some time ago, I visited a friend of mine. He was a man who had often helped me. When I could not understand something in the Bible, he told me what it meant. He knew a great deal. He knew the Lord. However, there was one strange thing—he was afraid to die.

Now I had heard that he was very ill, so I went to him, thinking that I must try to help him so that he would no longer be afraid to die. It was possible that that moment would soon come. It would be such a pity if he should be afraid, since he had known the Lord for such a long time. I prayed in my heart, "Oh, Lord Jesus, will You touch him, will You take away all fear from his heart?"

When I entered his room, he looked very happy. I asked him, "Are you a little better?"

"No," he said, "I'm very weak and I know that I must die. But what I'm so very happy about is that Jesus said, 'I give My sheep life eternal!' It is good He said it, for I cannot do anything myself. I am so tired that I cannot think properly, but I know that He will take care of me—even . . . even now. I cannot do it, but He is able."

How good it was to see that all the fear had disappeared. The Lord Himself takes care of His own. When there are moments that are difficult, we do not have to fear anything, for He is able to help us. He is faithful. He loves us.

Yes, He gives, and all that we have to do is accept! Not one of our prayers is lost. All our prayers are kept in heaven.

Another angel came and stood at the altar, having a golden censer; and there was given unto him much incense, that he should offer it with the prayers of all saints upon the golden altar which was before the throne.

Revelation 8:3

18
Little Angel

━━━━━━ ∽∽∽∽∽ ━━━━━━

In a children's hospital, I stood with my hand in a mother's hand. Her little girl had died. She looked like a little angel. On that little girl's dead face there was such an expression of peace!

"Oh, what joy it must be for that little child to be with Jesus! She will be so happy in heaven."

"I believe that too," the mother said, "but Corrie, you don't know how wounded I am. I loved my little girl so very much. Why did the Lord take her away from me?"

"I do not know, but God knows. He understands you. He loves you, and He loves that little girl."

There are moments when the suffering is so deep that one can hardly talk to a person. What a joy it is then to know that the Lord understands. No pit is so deep that the Lord is not deeper still. Underneath us are the everlasting arms—and the Lord understands.

> He shall cover thee with his feathers, and under his wings shalt thou trust: his truth shall be thy shield and buckler.
>
> Psalm 91:4

19
The Lost Sheep

Recently I met someone who had known the Lord for a long time, but she had turned away from Him. I sang to her, "What a Friend We Have in Jesus."

"I sang that song when I was in Sunday school," she said. "Yes, then I heard about the Lord Jesus every Sunday, but I have gone astray. I did not speak to Him and I did not listen to Him for many years. And now I'm so ill—what can I do?"

I told her of the good shepherd who had one hundred sheep, and one of them had also gone astray. "It did not come home with the others. That shepherd left the ninety-nine at home and went to seek that one silly sheep that had lost its way. He found it, took it in his arms, and brought it home. He was very, very happy. So Jesus is on His way looking for you. Won't you let yourself be found by this wonderful Friend who is our Savior?

He is looking for you, and when you call Him, He will take you and carry you home. He will be so happy!"

She closed her eyes and thought about it. Then, opening her eyes again, she said, "Is it as simple as all that?"

"Yes, it is."

She folded her hands. "Lord Jesus, forgive me for having gone my own way. Take me in Your arms and take me back home. Amen."

He was so near that it was as if we heard Him say, "Him that cometh to me I will in no wise cast out" (John 6:37).

She looked up and smiled a very happy smile. "What a Friend we have in Jesus!"

20
Worry

―――――― ∞∞ ――――――

"Oh, my children! My husband! How can they live without me?"

I was in a hospital in a large town in the United States, and my friend Ann was very ill. She knew it, and she did not tell me about her suffering but about the greatest worry she had. "Just imagine that I should die— who would take care of my family?" I held her hand in mine and just prayed for her. Then suddenly, I remembered a little poem.

Said the Robin to the Sparrow:
  "I should really like to know
Why these anxious human beings
  Rush around and worry so."

Said the Sparrow to the Robin:
  "Friend, I think that it must be
That they have no heavenly Father
  Such as cares for you and me."

Elizabeth Cheney

The Bible tells us, "Consider the ravens: for they neither sow nor reap; which neither have storehouse nor barn; and God feedeth them" (Luke 12:24). Aren't you much more valuable to Him than they are? Can any one of you, however much he worries, make himself an inch taller? And why do you worry about clothes? Consider how the flowers grow. They neither work nor weave, but I tell you that even Solomon in all his glory was never arrayed like one of these. Now, if God so clothes the flowers of the field which are alive today and discarded tomorrow, is He not much more likely to clothe you— you of little faith? Don't worry at all, then, about tomorrow. Tomorrow can take care of itself. One day's trouble is enough for one day (see Luke 12:25–28).

I could easily understand that her children and her husband were reasons to worry about the future. However, our times are in God's hands, and He loves her family even more than she loved them. Worrying is carrying tomorrow's load with today's strength— carrying two days at once. It is moving into tomorrow ahead of time. Worrying does not empty tomorrow of its sorrow—it empties today of its strength.

"Do you know, Ann, I do not believe that worry is from the Lord. It is from the enemy. There has been a man upon the earth of whom Satan is afraid, a man whom he can neither touch nor resist—Jesus Christ. And that is why we can go to Him for help. You are not able to overcome worry, but the Lord Jesus can, and He will—through His Holy Spirit. When we see that worry is a sin—and that is what it really is, for the Bible tells us not to worry—then we know what to do with sin, don't we?"

"Yes, we take it to the Lord, and when we confess our sins, the blood of Jesus cleanses us from all of our sins."

"That is true, so just ask forgiveness for having worried, and then ask Jesus to keep worry away. He gives us peace under all circumstances. I have a little stick here that cannot stand on my hand by itself. But I can let it stand even on the top of my finger, if my hand holds it. In the same way, we cannot keep worry away, but when we surrender to the wounded hands of Jesus, He keeps us from falling. One day He will present us blameless and with unspeakable joy. That will be on the day when He will reveal Himself. Jesus is stronger than all of our problems."

I prayed with Ann and then she said, "I have much to think about and I know one thing—I am not able, but Jesus is. He will do the job."

> Cast thy burden upon the LORD, and he shall sustain thee: he shall never suffer the righteous to be moved.
>
> Psalm 55:22

21
Our Times Are in God's Hands

It is a feast for me to be in Holland, for I meet friends of former days. I gather them in my home to tell them how much I have experienced during the last year. At one of these gatherings, I missed one of my friends. Somebody told me, "She is ill, so she could not come."

I went to see her. She told me what had happened. "I have been very ill, and everyone—myself too—thought I had to die. Oh, Corrie, I was not afraid. I was just thinking about the joy of seeing the Lord Jesus as I read in the Bible all the promises that speak of heaven. But then I began to recover. I am not strong, but the doctor said that in a short while I shall be able to do my work again."

"Are you happy?"

"Yes. I can be an eternity in heaven, and there is much work for me to do here in this world. I believe I will return to my everyday life richer than I was before I was ill. I see now that our times are in God's hands. I believe I will take the good opportunities, which the Lord will give me in the future, with more thankfulness, because I had thought I had lost them forever. I knew when I was dying how serious my condition was, but the Lord gave me grace. I was not afraid. Now I know, as I go back to my everyday life, that I will see the smaller problems in the light of eternity. I am sure I will not be so concerned about the problems of everyday life. I thank God that I had this illness. It made me more ready for life."

All things work together for good to them that love God.

Romans 8:28

The Lord never makes a mistake. One day, when we are in heaven, I'm sure we shall see the answers to the *whys*. My, how often I have asked, "Why?" In heaven we shall see God's side of the embroidery. God has no problems—only plans. There is never panic in heaven.

22
When I Saw Death

When I heard that my father had died in prison, I was alone in a cell. The prisoner who had been in the cell before me had written on the wall, NOT LOST, BUT GONE BEFORE.

After the first shock, I realized what a great joy it was for Father to be with the Lord in the beautiful place that Jesus had prepared for him. Straight from the cell in a prison to that place of peace and love of God. I could thank the Lord that He had taken him home. Yes, he was not lost but gone before.

When I saw Betsie after she had died in the ward of the concentration camp, I saw an expression of intense joy and peace on her face. She even looked young. I could only thank and praise the Lord that He had taken her to Himself. It was as if her face reflected a little bit of the tremendous joy that her soul experienced at that moment, when she went to be with the Lord.

I looked death in the eyes several times myself, and when fear came into my heart, I told the Lord Jesus. He did not give me a spirit of fear, but of power and of love and of a sound mind. I knew that I did not have to pass through the valley of the shadow of death alone. Jesus was with me.

The moment I was almost sure that death was coming was when my number was called out when we were standing on roll call. I had to stand as number one in the front row. Many of us thought—also I myself—that we had been called out because they were going to kill us.

I stood there for three hours, and next to me was a Dutch girl I had never seen before. I said to myself, *This is now the last person on earth to whom I can bring the gospel.* And I did. She told me her life story. I told her that Jesus loved her and that He had given His life on the cross to bear her punishment. That girl said yes to Jesus.

I was not killed; I was set free.

What do you think about death, about the death of your loved ones, and of yourself? Study the Bible. The answer is there. Talk with the Lord. He understands and loves you. When you come to Him, He will in no wise cast you out or send you away. Are you afraid? Give your fear to Him.

23

Are You Afraid to Die?

In Chicago I met an old friend of mine. I had not seen him for a long time, and I was spending only one day in his town. We had a good talk together, and I remember that I asked him a question. "Are you afraid to die?"

"Yes, I am," he said.

His answer surprised me. He loved the Lord and had known Him a long time. He had a deep faith in God. "Why are you afraid to die? You have been a Christian as long as I have known you. Surely you know that Jesus will not leave you alone for one moment."

"I am afraid, Corrie, because I have never died before. I am afraid because I do not know what it is like to die."

Then we talked about Jesus. Before He went to the cross, He had never died either. Was He also a little afraid?

But today Jesus knows what it is like to die. He has already been through death, and today Jesus says to you and to me, "I will never leave you nor forsake you," and "Lo, I am with you always." That means *even* death.

The old man smiled and said, "Isn't God good to us—that we could talk and think together about this today?"

Are you afraid to die?

Fear thou not; for I am with thee: be not dismayed; for I am thy God: I will strengthen thee; . . . yea, I will uphold thee with the right hand of my righteousness.

Isaiah 41:10

No temptation has overtaken you that is not common to man. God is faithful, and he will not let you be tempted beyond your strength, but with the temptation will also provide the way of escape, that you may be able to endure it.

1 Corinthians 10:13 RSV

PART 2

He Sets the Captive Free

24

I Was in Prison

⚜

"Name?" the interrogator inquired.

"Cornelia ten Boom, and . . ."

"Age?"

"Fifty-two."

It was a dark night when we were finally marched out of the building. We could see before us a large canvas-roofed army truck. The truck had no springs, and we bounced roughly over the bomb-pitted streets of The Hague. Leaving the downtown section, we seemed to be headed west, toward the suburbs of Scheveningen. Now we knew our destination: the federal penitentiary named after this seaside town of Scheveningen.

We turned left into an endless world of steel and concrete.

"Ten Boom, Cornelia!"

Another door rasped open. The cell was deep and narrow, scarcely wider than the door. A woman lay on the single cot, three others on straw ticks on the floor. "Give this one the cot," the matron said. "She's sick."

Soon I was moved to another location. The cell was identical to the one I had just left: six steps long, two wide, a single cot at the back. But this cell was empty. As the guard's footsteps died away down the corridor, I leaned against the cold metal of the door. Alone. Alone behind these walls . . . solitary!

Weeks later, "Get your things together! Get ready to evacuate!" The shouts of the guards echoed up and down the long corridor. I was thankful to see other faces again, but . . .

Where would we be taken? Where were we headed? One thing I dreaded . . . please . . . not into Germany!

Hours passed as the loaded train sat on the siding. It must have been two or three in the morning when the train at last began to move. The thought uppermost in every mind was: Is it Germany?

Finally, we seemed to stop in the middle of a wood. Floodlights mounted in trees lit a broad rough-cleared path lined by soldiers with leveled guns.

Spurred on by the shouts of the guards, I started up the path between the gun barrels. "Close ranks! Keep up! Five abreast!"

The nightmare march lasted a mile or more, when at last we came to a barbed wire

fence surrounding a row of wooden barracks. We went into one of them and fell
into an exhausted sleep. So began our stay
in this place that we learned was named
Vught, after the nearest small village. Vught
had been constructed in Holland by the
occupation army primarily as a concentration camp for political prisoners.

Several months later we were moved to
another camp. After a night punctuated with
the hail of bullets and machine-gun fire, we
learned at dawn that we were passing
through a border town into Germany. For
two more incredible days and nights we were
carried deeper and deeper into the land of
our fears.

From the crest of the hill, we saw a vast
scar on the green German landscape; a city
of low gray barracks, surrounded by concrete
walls on which guard towers rose at inter-
vals. In the very center a square smokestack
emitted a thin gray vapor into the blue sky.

"Ravensbrück!"

Like a whispered curse, the word passed
back through the lines. This was the noto-
rious extermination camp for women, whose
name we had heard even in Holland.

Adapted from *The Hiding Place*

25
Why I Was Sent to Prison

━━━━━━ ❦ ━━━━━━

I want to tell you about my experiences in three prisons. During World War II, I was a prisoner of the Gestapo because my family, my friends, and I had saved the lives of Jewish people in Holland. Adolf Hitler was preparing to kill all of them, and our task was to help them escape to safer countries.

When that was no longer possible, we hid them in our houses. In the end we had a group of eighty people with whom we worked to supply the desperate needs of a hidden people: food, clothing, houses, burials. There were many other factors facing a group of helpless persons hiding in a country already stripped by the occupying army of a powerful enemy.

We were betrayed and all were arrested. My father was eighty-four years old and lived only a short while in the prison where all his children and a grandson were also incarcerated. We never saw him again, for the prison walls separated us.

Father was a courageous man, but he understood that he was too old for prison life. "If I am imprisoned, I shall die, but it will be an honor for me to give my life for God's chosen people, the Jews," he said before they arrested him. I heard much later that he had died after only ten days' imprisonment.

26
Solitary Confinement

~~~~~

For the first week, they put me in a cell with four or five others, for I was very ill with pleurisy. The prison doctor said it would develop into tuberculosis, so I was sent to solitary confinement. He didn't want me to infect the others.

For the first time ever, I was really alone, and I knew my life was completely in the hands of the enemy. They could kill me or torture me or just forget about me altogether, and there would be no one to know or care.

At night the sounds of distant bombing penetrated the thick walls—and from somewhere within came the muffled cries of people being tortured by the Gestapo—that was a little bit of hell! When I lost courage, I tried singing, but the guards pounded on the door and demanded silence. They threatened to take me to the *dark* cell. In the dark cell you had to stand in water. Time became a very thick thing that I struggled to wade through.

Solitary confinement lasted four months. It wasn't only the isolation that was so hard, but the constant threat that at any moment of the day or night they would come for me. Whenever I heard footsteps outside my cell I would ask myself, "Are they coming to torture or kill me?"

Once I stood with my back against the wall with my hands spread out, as if to try to push away the walls that were closing in on me. I was dead scared. I cried out, "Lord, I'm not strong enough to endure this. I don't have the faith!"

Suddenly I noticed an ant, which I had watched roaming the floor of the cell for days. I had just mopped the floor with a wet rag, and the moment the ant felt the water on the stones, he ran straight to his tiny hole in the wall.

Then it was as if the Lord said to me, "What about that ant? He didn't stop to look at the wet rag or his weak feet—he went straight to his hiding place. Corrie, don't look at your faith; it is weak, like the tiny feet of that ant. Don't dwell on the treatment you might receive from these cruel people. I am your hiding place, and you can come running to Me just like that ant disappeared into that hole in the wall."

That brought real peace into my heart. I was then fifty-three years old, and I had always known about Jesus, but there in solitary confinement I began to really understand and experience for myself that His light is stronger than the deepest darkness.

I know there are moments for you when you lose all courage. You feel as a prisoner that you don't exist in the eyes of the people around you, in the eyes of God, or in your own eyes. Then you can read in the Bible a promise from Jesus: "Come to me, all you who are weary and burdened, and I will give you rest" (Matt. 11:28 NIV). When you can believe that, you will *know* Someone is still interested in you. Someone still cares about you—not as a number, but as a person.

27
The Interrogation

──────── ❧ ────────

After two months in the cell, I was called in for interrogation. The judges, the *Sachbearbeiters*, had a tremendous amount of power, and you had no rights whatsoever. They could give you a short sentence, a long sentence, or sentence you to death. You were totally in their hands.

I will never forget the moment when I was brought before my judge. I knew that not only was my own life in his hands, but I could incriminate many friends and coworkers. If I were forced to tell about them, it could mean their death sentence too.

I prayed for wisdom to answer all the questions of the interrogator, and there were *many* questions! I had to give my whole life history, even what I did in my spare time.

I told him that I taught a Bible class for feebleminded people who could not go to church because they could not understand sermons. "They need the Lord Jesus just as much as you and I do," I said to this National Socialist judge.

He replied, "What a waste of time! Isn't there far more value in converting a normal person than an abnormal one?"

My answer was, "If you knew Jesus, you would know that He has a great love for everyone who is despised or in need. It is possible that a poor, feebleminded child has more value in His eyes than you and I together."

He was angry when I said that, and he called the policemen, saying, "Take her back to her cell."

The next day I was brought again before my judge, who said, "I could not sleep during the night. I was thinking over what you had said about Jesus. I don't know anything about Him. We have plenty of time for the interrogation. First, tell me what you know about Jesus."

Boy, was that an opportunity! I began, "Jesus is a light come into this world. No one who believes in Him remains in darkness. Is there darkness in your life?"

His answer was, "Darkness? There is no light at all in my life. I hate my work. My wife is in Bremen, Germany. I don't even know if she is still alive. The town is being bombed heavily every night now. It is possible that she was killed this very night."

Suddenly the contact between us was on a totally different level. He was no longer the judge, but simply a man in great need, and I, his prisoner, could give him real encouragement as I brought him the gospel.

I said to him, "Jesus once said, 'Come to me, all who are heavy laden, and I will give you rest.' Come to me—*all*. That means you too. Come unto Jesus and He will give you rest. Tell Him your sins. He has never sent away any sinner."

I had a good talk with that man, and from then on he was no longer my enemy but my friend. He helped to save my life and did his utmost, though unsuccessfully, to set me free.

Of course, he still had to do his job, and so he showed me papers found in my house. To my horror I saw names, addresses, and particulars, which could mean not only *my* death sentence but the death of my family and my friends as well.

"Can you explain these papers?" he asked.

"No, I cannot." I felt miserable. (You will say, "Why did you have such dangerous papers in your house?" In our underground

efforts to save Jewish people, I worked with
many young people who did remarkably
courageous work. But they were not always
careful, so these papers were found in my
house.)

The judge knew even better than I how
dangerous those papers were. Suddenly he
turned around, opened the door of the stove,
and threw all the papers into the stove. At
that moment it was as if I understood for
the first time the text in Colossians 2:13–14:

> God has now made [you] to share in the
> very life of Christ! He has forgiven you all
> your sins: he has utterly wiped out the writ-
> ten evidence of broken commandments
> which always hung over our heads, and has
> completely annulled it by nailing it to the
> cross (PHILLIPS).

In heaven there are dangerous papers for
us all, and whether we believe it or not, we
will have to come before the judgment seat
of God. If we have refused Jesus Christ in
this life, then the judgment day will be terrible. But if we have received Jesus as our
Savior and Lord, then we have nothing to
fear, because Jesus nailed these terrible
papers to the cross when He died for the

sins of the whole world—your sins and mine. That is what I understood when I saw those papers destroyed by the flames in that stove.

Years later I met that judge in Germany, and I asked him, "Did you bring your sins to Him? It says in the Bible, 'If you confess your sins, He is faithful and just to forgive you, and He will cleanse you from all unrighteousness.'"

His answer was, "No, I did not do that. I am a very good man, and I have never committed sins."

"I am sorry you think that, because that means you cannot have salvation. Jesus will never ever send away anybody who comes to Him. But there is one kind of person in the Bible that I must tell you about. That was the Pharisee who said, 'I am good.' And Jesus could not and would not help him. If the time comes when you know you have sins, that you are a sinner, don't forget what I told you. The Bible tells us that Jesus has accepted our punishment at the cross, and the only thing we have to do is to receive Him as our Savior and come to Him and confess our sins."

He thought a moment and then suddenly said, "I know a sin that I have done."

I said, "All right—bring it to the Lord at once. Ask His forgiveness and thank Him for His forgiveness." He did.

Later in the evening he said, "I see another sin in my life."

"So, you know that you are a sinner. That is good. Just bring it to the Lord and ask forgiveness," I replied. When for the *fourth* time he remembered a sin that needed to be brought to the Lord, I knew he was ready to receive the Lord Jesus Christ as his Savior.

I said, "Now you can accept Jesus. You know that you need Him."

He did, and I know that his sins were forgiven and that his name was written in the Book of Life.

28
Ravensbrück

The Nazis were emptying jails everywhere! Male prisoners were sent in one division, and women prisoners in another. My sister Betsie and I, herded together with thousands of other women, were marched into Ravensbrück. It was called a work camp.

When we first came into this concentration camp, they took all our possessions. It was a real miracle that I was able to keep my Bible.

At great risk, I hid it on my back under my dress, and I prayed, "Lord, will You send Your angels to surround me?" Then I thought, *But angels are spirits, and you can see through spirits. I don't want these people to see me!* So I prayed then, in great fear, "Let Your angels *not* be transparent. Let them cover me."

And God did it! As we passed through the inspection, the woman in front of me was searched, then my sister, directly behind me, was searched—but I walked through unsearched!

Our barrack was built for four hundred women, but they packed fourteen hundred of us inside. Bunks were stacked all the way to the ceiling, and we each had a sleeping space only a few inches wide. When they were all working, we had eight toilets for the entire barracks!

In Ravensbrück it was dangerous to use the Word of God. If you were caught teaching the Bible, you were killed in a cruel way, but the guards never knew that I had a Bible meeting twice each day in Barrack 28. The one jammed room was filthy, crawling with fleas and lice, and the guards never came inside the door. You see how the Lord used both angels and lice to keep my Bible in our possession?

29

Does He Forget Me?

———— ⟨⟨⟨⟨⟩⟩⟩⟩ ————

Sometimes I experienced moments of great despair. I remember one night when I was outside the barrack on my way to roll call. The stars were beautiful. I remember saying, "Lord, You guide all those stars. You have not forgotten them but You have forgotten Betsie and me."

Then Betsie said, "No, He has not forgotten us. I know that from the Bible. The Lord Jesus said, 'I am with you always, until the end of the world,' and Corrie, He is here with us. We must believe that. It is not what we are *feeling* that counts but what we believe!"

> Feelings come and feelings go
>   and feelings are deceiving.
> My warrant is the Word of God,
>   none else is worth believing.

I slowly learned not to trust in myself or my faith or my feelings but to trust in Him.

Feelings come and go—they are deceitful. In all that hell around us, the promises from the Bible kept us sane.

Ravensbrück certainly *was* a work camp. It was the enemy's plan to work us—to death! Before the war ended, ninety-six thousand women died there. Even my dear Betsie became an old woman before my eyes and slowly starved to death.

The smoke from the crematorium was like a black haze over the camp. Every day seven hundred women died or were killed. There were far too many of us, and death was the only solution to the problem. I looked death in the eye day after day, and I found the Lord to be my refuge still, my only hiding place.

30
The Lifeline

———— ✦ ————

The greatest moment of your life can be when everything seems finished for you. That is the moment when you lay your weak hand in the strong hand of Jesus. For Jesus can make life and death—present and future—victorious! He can give you eternal life; not only life in heaven, but life right now.

It is as when you have fallen in the sea and you think, *Now I will surely drown. I can swim perhaps an hour, but then I will sink!* A lifeline is the only thing that can help you then.

I found that when you are drowning in the terrific misery of the world, Jesus is everything for you—your only lifeline. When you think you have lost everything, then you can be *found* by Jesus Christ.

He died for you, He lives for you, and He loves you more than any human being can

love. I have told people about Him for thirty-
three years, in sixty-four countries, and in
all that time nobody has ever told me he was
sorry he asked Jesus to come into his life.
You won't be sorry either.

31
A Storm Laid Down

Punishments were often general in Ravensbrück. Once we suddenly heard shouting, beating, and swearing in our room. We lived in a crowded room, packed together. Everything was filthy and broken-down. Two people were sharing a very small bunk, and one had thrown the other out of the cot, so they started to fight.

Betsie said, "Corrie, we need to pray. This is dangerous!"

It *was* dangerous. If the guards had heard the fighting in our barrack, we would all have been cruelly punished. Betsie remained praying. She prayed and prayed. It was as if a storm died down. We heard less beating, less swearing and shouting. Finally, it was quiet, and Betsie said, "Thank You, Father. Amen."

Now do you see what happened there? There was a room with many prisoners in great danger, and there was one starving old woman—Betsie. God used Betsie to save the situation. That is what God is willing to do and is going to do with you and me when we let Him show us what to do—when He guides us.

The Bible says that we are representatives of heaven on this earth, that we are ambassadors of Jesus Christ. It is terribly important for the world that there are ambassadors—representatives from heaven—in this world, and you and I can be those ambassadors. Often it will save the situation and bless our surroundings. Because we do it so well? No, not at all. Because the Lord is using us to do what *He* wants done.

32
No Wilderness, the Lord's Garden

"You must tickle the hand of God before He is willing to help you," said a prisoner who was sitting on the bed behind me.

"No, girl, that is not true. When you really know the Lord, you know that He is far more ready to bless us than we are ready to ask for His blessing. He loves us. The Bible says, 'You are God's field'" (1 Cor. 3:9 RSV). The great preacher and writer C. H. Spurgeon expresses this very clearly:

> Oh, to have one's soul as a field under
> heavenly cultivation,
> No wilderness, but a garden of the
> Lord, walled around by grace,
> Planted by instruction, visited by love,
> Weeded by heavenly discipline, guarded
> by divine power.
> One's soul thus favored is prepared to
> yield fruit unto the glory of God.

A garden does not do much. It does bring forth fruit and flowers. But the one who has the responsibility is the gardener, and it is He, our Gardener, who blesses us, surrounds us with grace, and disciplines us. Whether we are willing or not, He does the job. On our part it is necessary to surrender, and then He makes His garden from the wilderness of our lives. It is wonderful what He is willing and able to do.

33
Is Forgiveness Possible?

———— ❧❧❧ ————

Do you know how it feels when your heart is full of hatred? We were working in an area where wrecked airplanes were piled together. We had to gather the many pieces and load them onto big trucks. It was terribly heavy work for us.

My sister Betsie was a very frail woman, and she could not lift much, but she did her utmost. Suddenly one of the guards noticed that Betsie was picking up only the little pieces, because the big pieces were too heavy for her.

Betsie said kindly to her, "Don't give me more to do than I am trying to do already, because I am not strong enough to lift these heavy parts."

The woman guard said, "You don't decide what you do. *I* decide." Suddenly the guard started to brutally beat Betsie. I have never been so enraged! The other prisoners held me back so I could not grab the guard.

When she had gone, I ran to Betsie, who had blood all over her face. She said, "No, don't hate, Corrie. You must love and forgive."

"I cannot! I am not able."

If there is hate in your heart, you cannot forgive. I knew this, and I also knew that Jesus had said, "But if you do not forgive, neither will your Father which is in heaven forgive your trespasses" (Mark 11:26).

After we were back in our barrack, I climbed out of the window and went for a little walk alone, and I talked with the Lord. I said, "Lord, I cannot forgive that brutal woman. It is more difficult to forgive when people you love suffer than when you suffer yourself."

Then the Lord reminded me of a text. I had my little Bible hidden under my dress. I opened it and read, "God's love has been poured into our hearts through the Holy Spirit which has been given to us" (Rom. 5:5 RSV).

Suddenly I saw that what *I* was not able to do, the Lord, in me, was able to do. I said, "Oh, Lord, I thank You for Romans 5:5. I thank You, Jesus, that You brought into my heart God's love through the Holy Spirit.

Thank You, Father, that Your love in me is stronger than my hatred."

At that moment, when I was able to forgive, my hatred disappeared. What a liberation! Forgiveness is the key that unlocks the door of resentment and the handcuffs of hatred. It is a power that breaks the chains of bitterness and the shackles of selfishness. What a liberation it is when you can forgive. Here again we see that we are not a wilderness but a garden of the Lord, when we give our lives to Jesus. He does the job.

34
Lizzy

━━━━━━━━ ✿ ━━━━━━━━

We had to live in beds stacked one on top of another. There were three beds in each stack, and above the cots where my sister Betsie and I slept, there lived a girl, Lizzy, who was a prostitute. Every day Betsie gathered the people around us, and she or I gave a little Bible talk. Lizzy did not join us, but she always listened, and once I heard Betsie talking with her.

"I do not know if I can come to Jesus," Lizzy said to Betsie.

"Why not? The Lord loves you. You are very precious in God's eyes, and when you come to Jesus, He will not send you away. He has never sent anyone away who came to seek forgiveness and to find the answer for his sin or guilt problem.

"God made this world good, and human beings were without sin, but then we people started to do wrong things, and God had to punish us. But He loved us so much that He had a talk with His Son, Jesus, and God said, 'What must I do? I have to punish people, but I love them.'

"Jesus said, 'Father, I will go to the world, and I will carry their punishment.' And the Father agreed. Jesus came to this world and He lived here for thirty-three years. That must have been a difficult time for Him, even from the beginning, for He was used to being in heaven, and then He came to such a dark world, full of problems.

"The most terrible thing He experienced was when He was crucified. Crucifixion is a very cruel, torturous way to kill people. He could have been saved from that. There were many angels around Him, and had Jesus told them to keep Him from the cross, they would have done so. But He did not ask them, because He was willing to suffer and die. It was His purpose, when He came into this world, to die for your sins and mine.

"Now when we believe in Him we do not have to fear any punishment. We are free! There will be a judgment day, and every one of us will be present there, but we have nothing to fear when we believe in the Lord Jesus Christ. There is no condemnation for those who belong to Him. And Jesus Himself is our Judge and Advocate. You can read that in the Bible."

> Who then will condemn us? Will Christ? No! For he is the one who died for us and came back to life again for us and is sitting at the place of highest honor next to God, pleading for us there in heaven.
>
> Romans 8:34 LB

"But I don't do what I should do!" said Lizzy.

"I don't believe that you must do anything," replied Betsie. "Believe in the Lord Jesus Christ and you will be saved. What had to be done has all been done by Jesus Christ. Your part is to accept that at the cross He died for your sins."

Lizzy folded her hands and said, "Thank You, Jesus, that You did it all at the cross. I surely am not able to do much to change myself, but I thank You that You will do it in me."

35
The Red Ticket

~~~~~~

"Fall in for the street commando!"

Making streets was heavy work. Betsie and I showed our red tickets, which we had just received from the *Aufseherin*. They were the sign that we were unable to do hard labor. We climbed on our cot and hummed a little song. We picked up the stockings, which we had to knit for the German soldiers.

"You seem to be happy," said the woman behind us.

"We certainly are. We were called to enroll in the street commando, and look what we have." We showed the red tickets.

The woman smiled cynically. "Do you know what your red tickets mean? At the first cleaning up of prisoners, all the red-ticket owners disappear into the gas chamber."

We stopped humming our song. I looked through the window at the smoke that was going up from the crematorium, and I

109

thought, *When will my time come to be killed?*

Betsie saw what I was looking at. "Are you afraid, Corrie?"

> Afraid? Of what?
> To feel the Spirit's glad release?
> To pass from pain to perfect peace?
> The strife and strain of life to cease?
> Afraid of that?

I knew that my sins were forgiven, that my name was in the Book of Life, and that I had received Jesus as my Savior. He had made me a child of God. Jesus gives eternal life. That means the life that belongs to eternity, to heaven. And I had that.

I knew that if they killed me I would go to the Father's house with many mansions. I looked death in the eyes. I saw the valley of the shadow of death. But I was not afraid, for I knew that I would not go alone through that valley. Jesus was going to take my hand and help me through.

How good to know that you belong to Jesus! Do you know it? If not, lay your hand in His strong hand. Those who come to Him, He will in no wise cast out.

36
Ask More—He Will Give

It was crowded and filthy and miserable in that room built for two hundred where seven hundred of us lived together. (There were two such rooms.) Although it was a terrible place, yet there were several things for which I was thankful.

One reason for gratitude was that twice a day Betsie or I could gather the prisoners around us for a little Bible message. First I did it only on Sunday, but when I saw that so many people died or were killed from one Sunday to the next, I decided to risk it every day.

Several of my fellow prisoners really came to the Lord and accepted the Lord Jesus as their Savior. They decided to come every day for the Bible message. Then I gave the talk in the evenings for those prisoners who were assigned to work elsewhere during the day and couldn't attend the daytime meetings in the area where I had to knit stockings.

When I finished teaching, there would be many questions, and I realized that many did not know the simplest truths of the Bible.

I often talked about the fact that when we pray, the Lord hears our prayers. He loves us and loves to have us talk to Him. He always listens when we pray. I told them about the miracles that actually happened to me when God answered my prayers. Sometimes He does not answer our prayers in the way we want or expect Him to answer. We will understand why one day when we are in heaven.

I told them the story of a blind man who came to Jesus during the time that Jesus was in the world with us. Jesus healed him, and then He asked the man, "Can you see?"

The man said, "I see men like trees walking." Jesus touched his eyes again, and the man said, "Now I can see clearly." (Read this in Mark 8:22–26.)

You know, sometimes when you first come to Jesus, it is as if you do not see so very much and you do not understand what is happening. You are not able to enjoy your new life. Then the best thing you can do is to tell the Lord that you do not understand it, that you do not see clearly, and that you really see man as the blind man did—like walking trees.

If Jesus had not asked this blind man whether he could see, I am sure that nevertheless the man would have told Him, and said, "Lord, I am glad that I can see a little bit, but I do not see enough." Then Jesus would have healed him.

So it is with you and me. If we do not see as much as we need or want to see, then we must tell it to the Lord. He will heal our eyes so that we see that the love of God is far greater than anything else.

There is an ocean of God's love that we discover when we receive Jesus Christ as our Savior. He shows it to us through His Holy Spirit. God sees you and me. He knows everything about us, and He loves us so much that He wants to help us and do what we ask.

37

Is a No *Answer an Answer?*

━━━━━━━━━ ❧ ━━━━━━━━━

When God gives us the *no* answer, it can be a difficult testing of our faith, but when we study the Bible, we understand more and more that God never makes a mistake. Once we are in heaven, we will understand it all.

My life is like a weaving between my
    God and me,
      I do not choose the colors, He work-
      eth steadily.
Ofttimes He weaveth sorrow and I in
    foolish pride,
      forget He sees the upper, and I the
      underside.

I once prayed for Betsie, my sister. She was so very ill. Even in the filthy bunk in our barrack or at our work, it was such a joy and comfort for us just to be together night and day. Now she was in that primitive hospital, and our friends and I, who loved her so, prayed that the Lord would heal her. But when I returned to the hospital after roll call and looked through the window, I saw that she had died. That was one of the darkest moments of my life.

I could not understand why God had not answered my prayer. A few days later, I was called out of lineup and I heard that I was to be set free. I had to go through the office on my way out, and I learned that they did not know my sister had died. I asked them, "What about my sister?" I wanted to find out what would have happened to her if she had still been alive.

They said, "Your sister must remain here for the duration of the war."

"May I remain with my sister?"

"Not for a minute! Now get out!"

I have praised and thanked my Lord for that unanswered prayer. Just imagine how it would have been if she had been healed and would have had to stay in the hell of Ravensbrück without me. I would have returned to my homeland tormented night and day by the consciousness of her suffering. I saw God's side of the embroidery.

38
Freedom

It was 3:30 A.M. I woke up, and my first thought was, *Roll call*. I looked around me. Clean windows, a chair, a table, a picture on the wall. I was no longer in prison. I was free!

I could sleep for several more hours, but I did not. I got up and started to write down what I had experienced in the three prisons. Those writings became my first book, *A Prisoner and Yet* . . . It became a best-seller in Holland, because people were interested in reading about what had happened to the victims of the concentration camps.

For many years of my life I had been the leader of Girl Guide clubs (European Girl Scouts). As soon as I recovered my strength a bit, I got together with all the girls I could locate to tell them what I had experienced and to find out what had happened to them.

116

After much talk together, they asked, "What are you going to do?" We were sitting in a clubhouse, cross-legged on the floor. My club girls were interested in all I had learned in prison—that difficult class in life's school.

"Girls, I'm so thankful that all my tomorrows are in God's hands. I want to tell you what happened one night." And this was what I told them:

It was midnight in Ravensbrück, and Betsie tried to wake me up. Sleep was such an important thing. You forgot that you were in prison.

"Why are you waking me up? Leave me, please, in the world of dreams, where there are no guards, no barbed wire, and no lice."

Betsie put her coat over our heads so that we could talk without disturbing our fellow prisoners. "I have to talk with you, Corrie. God has told me several things that we must do after the war, and I am afraid that I may forget some of His instructions.

"We have learned so much here, and now we must go all over the world to tell people what we now know—that Jesus' light is stronger than the deepest darkness. Only prisoners can know how desperate this life is. We can tell from experience that no pit is too deep, because God's everlasting arms always sustain us.

"We must rent a concentration camp after the war, where we can help displaced Germans to get a roof over their heads. I have heard that 95 percent of the houses in Germany are bombed out. No one will want these concentration camps after the war, so we must rent one and help the German people find a new life in a destroyed Germany. God has shown me in a vision, a house in Holland in which we will receive the Dutch prisoners who survive the concentration camps. We will help them to find their way through life again."

I asked her, "Must we stay in that camp, which we will open for the people here in Germany, or will we be able to stay in the house for the ex-prisoners, at home in Holland?"

"Neither," Betsie said. "You must travel all over the world and tell everybody who will listen what we have learned here—that Jesus is a reality and that He is stronger than all the powers of darkness. Tell them. Tell everyone who will listen! He is our greatest Friend, our hiding place."

A week later Betsie died. A week after that I was set free, and only one week later, the

Germans put to death all the women of my age in Ravensbrück.

I looked at my Girl Guides who had listened to my story. "Girls," I said, "I know that you are sincerely interested in what I am going to do. My answer is that I will obey all the instructions that God gave to me through Betsie."

I obeyed. You can read about many of my adventures over the years in my book *Tramp for the Lord*.

Since I have often visited in prisons, now I want to talk with you about some of these experiences.

39
Kimio

While visiting a prison in Africa, I heard about a young man who was sentenced to die. I asked to see him, but the prison officials would allow me to enter his cell only if three soldiers went in with me.

The cell had a very high ceiling and one small window at the top for light. It was bare, except for a shelf very low to the ground. Sitting on that shelf was a handsome black African who had one more week to live. I was praying very hard! I wanted to be able to talk with him as if we were alone, but the soldiers made me uncomfortable. I always reacted that way when I was around men with guns.

As we talked, I learned that the young man's name was Kimio and that he had a wife and children. Kimio knew about the cross and that Jesus had died there for the sins of the whole world, including his sins.

I asked him if he knew who was responsible for his arrest and imprisonment. He was a political prisoner, and there came into his eyes the darkness of hatred.

"I can name every person responsible for my being here," he said.

"Can you forgive them?"

"No, I can't."

"I understand that. Once a man betrayed me and my whole family. Because of his betrayal, four of my family died in prison, and I suffered in three of the most horrible prisons in the whole world.

"And, Kimio, I could forgive that man. Not through my own strength—never—but through the Lord. The Holy Spirit can fill your heart with God's love, and He can give you the power to forgive. Kimio, I felt so free after I had forgiven that man. You have to die very soon."

"Yes, and I have a wife and children whom I will never see again because of those men."

"I understand, Kimio, but you have to come before God. You have to face a righteous God very soon, and you know about Jesus at the cross.

"Jesus said, 'If you do not forgive those who wrong you, my heavenly Father will not forgive you.' So Kimio, you *have* to forgive.

"You are unable, but the Holy Spirit in you *is* able. Just pray this prayer with me. 'Thank You, Jesus, that You have brought into my heart God's love through the Holy Spirit. Thank You, Father, that Your love in me is stronger than my hatred.'"

I don't remember what else Kimio and I talked about after that, but I no longer felt the presence of those three armed soldiers. There was the presence of angels in that cell. I learned later that Kimio wrote to his wife, "Love the people who have brought me here. Forgive them. You can't, and I can't, but Jesus *in* us is able."

Kimio was trapped by the misery of this world, but he learned how to be free.

40
Joy? Is That Possible?

———————— ✤ ————————

The worst prison I have ever seen was in another area of Africa. The building was too small for all the prisoners. Only half of them could go inside the building at night; the rest had to stay outside.

During the day they were all kept crammed together in the dirty compound in front of the prison. There had been a tropical rainstorm, and the ground was one large pool of mud. I saw that some men had branches on which they were sitting. Some had small pieces of paper, and others had little shelves. They had all struggled to find something to sit on. Everything was dark and black, but the darkest was the expression of their faces.

I often pray at the same time I am speaking, saying one thing to the Lord and another to the people who are listening to my talk. On this day I said, "Lord give me a message

for these men that will help them in this very
difficult place where they live."

The answer from the Lord was, "What is
the fruit of the Spirit?" I knew it: "The fruit
of the Spirit is love, joy, peace, patience,
kindness, goodness, faithfulness, gentleness,
self-control" (Gal. 5:22 RSV).

Then the Lord said, "Speak about joy."

"Lord, how can I speak about joy to these
people who live in this terrible place?"

The answer was, "My Holy Spirit is here
in this place, and the fruit of the Spirit is
available wherever you are."

Then I remembered that when I had been
in prison I had found joy even in the midst
of the most desperate surroundings. When
we are powerless to do a thing, it is a great
joy that we can come and step inside the
ability of Jesus.

"Lord," I said, "You are able to give joy."
Then I heard myself giving a very happy message. The faces of the men lit up when I told
them that the joy of the Lord can be our
strength, even when we are in very difficult
circumstances.

The only thing necessary to begin moving into the joy of the Lord is to tell Jesus
Christ that you would like to be His follower.

"Receive Jesus Christ as your Savior and Lord, and He will give you the joy," I said.

Many did. I could see it in their faces. But I also saw faces of people who were not ready or willing. They remained just as dark and unhappy as before.

I said to them, "Fellows, I can understand that you think such joy is not possible for you when you are in this prison, but I can tell you that I was in a prison far worse than yours, where only 20 percent of us came out alive. The rest all starved or were killed in a cruel way. But the Lord Jesus was with us. His Holy Spirit was in our hearts, and there was often a great joy.

"There is joy for you too, but you must be at peace with God and man—that *is* possible! When you confess your sins to the Lord, He is faithful and just, and He forgives you. He removes your sins, He cleanses your heart, and He fills you with the Holy Spirit. The fruit of the Spirit is joy."

Finally, I asked, "Who is willing to receive Jesus Christ? Raise your hand."

All the prisoners did, and even the guards who were there did too! Now, when *everyone* raises his hand to accept Jesus Christ, then I do not always trust it, but I looked into their faces and saw that this time it was real for all of them.

When I went to the car to leave for the next place, all the men and the guards accompanied me to the street. They were standing around the car, shouting something that I could not understand. I asked the missionary who was with me, "What are these men saying?"

She smiled and said, "They are shouting, 'Come again, old woman. Come again and tell us more about Jesus.'"

I was so glad! You know, I had to leave, but the Lord stayed with these men, and the Holy Spirit filled their hearts. It is true that when you lay your weak hand in the strong hand of Jesus, He keeps you from falling and never leaves you alone.

41
Three Decent Sinners

The apostle Paul was in prison. It must have been terrible for him. His hands were chained to the hands of two guards night and day. He never knew from one day to the next what the enemy was intending to do with him.

We do know some of the things that Paul did while a prisoner. He wrote letters, which you should read. Some of these epistles you should read are called Ephesians, Philippians, Colossians, and the two letters to Timothy.

Another thing we know about Paul is that he used his time in prison to bring the gospel to the people around him. These men to whom he was chained could not run away when he preached. And what was the result? People were converted! At the very end of his letter to the Philippian church, Paul writes, "Give my greetings in Christian fellowship to every one of God's people. The brothers here with me all send greetings. All the Christians here would like to send their best wishes, particularly those who belong to the emperor's household" (Phil. 4:21–22 PHILLIPS).

I once spoke about this in a prison in New Zealand, because I believe that every prisoner can help his fellow prisoners to know and receive Jesus Christ. Prisoners can be reached by their fellow prisoners better than by people from outside, because they understand one another.

I know some of you are thinking what some of the prisoners there in New Zealand thought, *Perhaps God can use other people, but not me. I am not good enough.*

Do you know what happened there? One of the prisoners suddenly stood up and said, "Fellows, this morning I read in the Bible about three murderers. One's name was Paul, one was Moses, and the other was David. We know them as heroes of God, but all three were murderers. What God can do with a totally surrendered murderer! There is hope for you and me, fellows!"

Yes, there is hope for you who read this. I believe I have never heard such a good sermon as that one from a man who was a prisoner. What God can do with you when you surrender all is *tremendous!* There is one condition: "Stay always within the boundaries where God's love can reach and bless you" (Jude 21 LB).

I have a glove. This glove cannot do anything, but when my hand is in the glove, the glove can do many things. It can drive a car, it can write.

Yes, I know, it is not the glove that does it, it is the hand inside the glove. You and I are—and Moses, David, and Paul were—just gloves. It was the Holy Spirit in them, and in you and me, who does the work.

What we have to do is to make room for the Holy Spirit, and then miracles can happen in our lives. Perhaps you think, *Oh, that is possible for a* mature *Christian, for somebody who knows the Bible well and has had training.* Perhaps you even think you must first go to a Bible school. All these things are good, but the Lord can also use you when you have none of these opportunities.

42
Hi, Brother!

————— ✦ —————

Let me tell you about a prisoner I met some years ago in Bermuda. I had spoken to a big group in the prison, and a black guard asked me, "Will you go with me to some cells where there are people who really need your advice?" I went into that part of the prison where the men were kept who were not even allowed to attend meetings.

I saw two men in a cell. One of them had a round, red tag on his back.

"Has that man tried to run away?" I asked the guard.

"Yes," he replied. "How do you know that?"

"Because of the red tag on the back of his uniform. I have been in three prisons, and we were also forced to wear red tags on our uniforms if we tried to run away."

"This man is a murderer, and he was sentenced to whippings. He was so afraid of the whippings that he tried to run away. Poor fellow, he has had a double portion."

When I saw him sitting there on the floor, the expression on his face reminded me of a wounded animal, and my heart went out to him. I prayed, "Lord, help me to find a way to his heart." I went to him with my Bible in my hand and asked him, "Say, fellow, have you had a whipping?"

"Yes."

"Was it bad?"

"Yes."

"Did they take you to the hospital afterward?"

"No, it was not that serious."

He stood up and came to the barred door, probably thinking to himself, "That woman is sure asking me strange questions!"

Then I asked, "Did they treat your wounds?"

"Yes, they did. They rubbed them."

"Is there hatred in your heart?"

"Hatred? My whole heart and my whole life are full of hatred."

"I can understand that."

"Ha! You?"

Then I told him how I had felt when they whipped my sister, because she was too frail and weak to shovel sand. How hatred had come into my heart!

But I said, "Fellow, a miracle happened then. Jesus brought into my heart God's love through the Holy Spirit, and I had no hatred. I could forgive.

"And when you receive Jesus Christ as your Savior, He will fill your heart—not with hatred but with love. How do you do it? You just come to Him and say, 'Lord Jesus, will You be my Savior?' The Lord is willing to be that. Then you must ask Him to come into your heart. And He *will* come, because it is written in the Bible, and the Bible is true. Jesus said, 'Behold, I stand at the door, and knock: if any man hear my voice, and open the door, I will come in to him' (Rev. 3:20).

"Fellow, when the Lord Jesus comes into your heart, there is love in your heart. The worst may happen in your life, but the best remains."

I prayed with that man, and then he prayed. I believe I had never heard such a strange prayer. The man had never prayed before, but one of the things he did was thank Jesus that He had died for him on the cross.

Have you ever thanked Jesus for that?

I shook hands with the man. Then he said, "Have you another five minutes?"

"Sure. Why?"

"On the other side of the corridor, in the third cell, is a man in great darkness. Please, tell him also of Jesus."

I went to the man in the third cell. I told him about Jesus, and how I prayed for him! When you speak about Jesus, you can always pray at the same time. You can have the vertical and the horizontal connection at the same moment.

The man in the third cell said his yes to Jesus. I mean a real yes—a decision.

I had to leave the prison then, but I first passed the cell of the murderer. "Say, fellow, that was good that you sent me to the third cell. He also has accepted Jesus Christ as his Savior and Lord."

The man looked around me and shouted across the corridor, "Hi, brother!" A babe in Christ, a few minutes old, and he already had a burden for souls. How old are you?

When someone becomes a Christian he becomes a brand new person inside. He is not the same any more. A new life has begun! All these new things are from God who brought us back to himself through what Christ Jesus did. And God has given us the privilege of urging everyone to come into his favor and be reconciled to him. For God was in Christ, restoring the world to himself, no longer counting men's sins against them but blotting them out. This is the wonderful message he has given us to tell others. We are Christ's ambassadors. God is using us to speak to you: we beg you, as though Christ himself were here pleading with you, receive the love he offers you—be reconciled to God.

2 Corinthians 5:17–20 LB

43
Corrie's Message

In New Zealand I visited a small prison, where there were probably no more than fourteen men. We had a good time together. The men were sitting with their backs against a wall, and I was sitting in front of them, speaking about the great joy of knowing that you are a child of God.

I told them that when you ask Jesus to come into your heart and you confess your sins, then He does a great miracle in your heart, which He Himself calls "being born into the family of God." At that time you may say to God, "Father, my Father." And He says to you, "My child."

Four of these men made a decision. Each wanted to give his heart to Jesus, to be cleansed and born into the kingdom of God—to be born a child of God.

Before I left, I shook hands with all the men. One was a very old man. He cried and held my hand and kissed it. I was a little bit amused about that and finally said, "Now,

friend, let me go, and the Lord bless you."
Then he let go of my hand.

This man was sentenced to a long imprisonment for the crime of manslaughter. The woman with whom he lived had snored one night when he was drunk. He strangled her because of her noise. When he realized that the woman was dead, he was so scared he ran straight to the police and told them, "I have murdered my wife."

"Why are you crying so?" I asked him.

He replied, "Because I am so happy. I have always had such terrible feelings of guilt because I killed the woman I lived with. Now I have brought it to the Lord Jesus, and I know I am forgiven. I am a child of God! Jesus is in my heart."

A year later I went back to that prison, and I talked with some of the men there. I asked where the old man was, and they told me, "He died some time ago."

One of the men took me aside and said, "I must tell you something. Whenever that man heard me going through the corridor, he called me into his cell. He would say, 'Let us talk about Corrie's message.'"

How happy I was that the Lord had used me to help that man!

44

Conversations in Prisons

━━━━ ◈ ━━━━

I know there are almost insurmountable problems when you are in prison. I would like to write about some of the problems we discussed when I talked with prisoners in America.

Ann

"What is the most difficult thing that you have to go through?" I asked Ann.

I sat with her in her cell in solitary confinement. She showed me a photograph of her husband and children. "Because of my crime, I have given them such a hard life. They lack a wife and mother, and they have to bear the shame—all because of the bad things I have done."

She told me that she had accepted Jesus as her Savior ten years ago but had solidly backslid. She knew much about the Bible, so it was easy to talk with her.

"There is an answer to your problem, Ann. It is Jesus. He has told us that we may pray for one another. You can pray for your children and your husband. You can tell the Lord everything. He understands you better than any human being.

"I read in the Book of Revelation that not one of our prayers is lost. They are kept in heaven. That is how important they are in our heavenly Father's eyes.

"You feel guilty that your family has to suffer because of you. You carry that guilt. I have a book here. It must lie somewhere: on my hand, on the table, or on the floor. It is the same with guilt. It must lie somewhere. It is lying on you. You are carrying it.

"Now the Bible teaches us a mystery. When Jesus died on the cross, God laid on Him the guilt of the whole world. Jesus was willing to bear that terrible death, to carry our sins, our guilt. You may bring your sins, your guilt to Jesus, and He will forgive you and make you clean. Then He will fill you with the Holy Spirit. The fruit of the Spirit is peace and joy and love. Then you will be able to think of your husband and children with peace."

Ann said, "I believe all you tell me, but I cannot accept it now. I have been away from the Lord for so long. Ten years ago I could have accepted it, but now it is too late."

"Ann, do you remember the story of the lost sheep? A shepherd had one hundred sheep. One evening when he came home, he saw that one sheep was lost. What did he do? He left the ninety-nine at home and went to look for that one lost sheep. He found it, took it on his shoulder, and brought it home.

"You are a lost sheep. Jesus will bring you home. The shepherd rejoiced and organized a feast to celebrate the finding of the lost sheep. Jesus rejoices when He finds you. Only tell Him everything. He loves you. Confess your sins to Him and ask Him to come into your heart. He will rejoice, and you will rejoice."

Ann did it. And I know Jesus rejoiced!

Frank

"Trust and study the Bible, Frank. It is the Word of God. You have asked Jesus to come into your life, and He came. Now all the promises of the Bible are yours."

Frank had seen one of Billy Graham's meetings on television, and he had joined the many who came to Jesus that evening.

"Do you know what my problem is when I read the Bible?" Frank said. "It all happened so very long ago. I have seen Christians who were really happy, but after a while they backslid. Their Christianity did not last long."

"Frank, what can help you and give you solid ground to stand on is your faith in Jesus. He is the same yesterday, today, and tomorrow. He never changes. He is the same now as He was in Israel two thousand years ago. He is a solid rock to stand upon.

On Christ the solid rock, I stand.
All other ground is sinking sand.

"Talk much with Him. He is here *now*. He loves and understands you."

Roger

He was a young man in a big prison. I had spoken in the chapel, and while he cleaned the table where we had had some refreshments, I had an opportunity to talk with him.

Without looking up, he said, "I am afraid."

"Who are you afraid of? The guards?"

"No, the men around me. They say that they will kill me if I do not do what they ask me to do. They tell me to do dirty things, which I cannot refuse."

"Roger, I was in a prison where the devil was strong, and I was afraid, like you are. I saw then that I was weak and the devil was stronger, much stronger than I. But then I saw Jesus, who is much stronger than the devil. Jesus and I together could overcome the devil. When I realized that, miracles happened.

"Paul, in the Bible, had a problem in his life. The Bible does not tell us exactly what it was, but he calls it a 'thorn in the flesh, messenger of Satan, to harass me.'

"You can read about it in 2 Corinthians 12:7–10. Paul asked God to take it away, but God did not remove that thing. He answered Paul, 'My grace is sufficient for you, for my power is made perfect in weakness.' God does not always remove difficult things from our lives, but His grace in us *is* sufficient to overcome the difficulties."

Have you got any rivers you think are
    uncrossable?
Got any mountains you can't tunnel
    through?
God specializes in things called impossible.
He can do what no other can do.

〜〜〜

"I am going on parole next week."

"Boy, that is good! Are you glad?"

"No, this was my fourth time in prison, and soon it will be my fifth. I know myself."

"No, Mike, Jesus has found you, you have found Jesus, and you and He together will overcome the temptations. Read the story of Gideon in Judges 6.

"Gideon was neither strong nor courageous. He hid himself in a barn, in the bottom of a winepress. But how did God see him? The angel who came to him said, 'The Lord is with you, you mighty man of valor.' Because the Lord was with him, Gideon changed from a weakling into a strong overcomer. The Lord said to him, 'Go in this your strength.'

"Mike, the devil is stronger—much stronger than you and me—but Jesus is much stronger than the devil, and with Jesus, we are stronger than the devil.

"It is important that you do what Jude said: 'Stay always within the boundaries where God's love can reach and bless you' (Jude 21 LB).

"If, when you leave prison, you go straight to a bar and get yourself drunk and renew your relationship with the friends who helped you to go to prison through their advice and assistance in your crimes, you can be sure that you will find yourself in this building for the fifth time. You stand on victory ground with Jesus, but you must be willing to go the whole way with Him. You are free to choose."

"That is exactly my problem. I am willing now to be a good guy, but what happens when I am free?"

"Mike, you are not the only one who has this problem, but the Lord knows that. The Bible supplies the answer when it says, 'Be filled with the Spirit' in Ephesians 5:18. A Spirit-filled Christian is a difficult target for the enemy, for he has the fruit of the Spirit and the gifts of the Holy Spirit, which are like a good armor and weapons in his hand. A compromise with the enemy is deadly dangerous, just as if a soldier on the front line helps the enemy to attack him and his fellow soldiers.

"If, again and again, you lay your weak hand in the strong hand of Jesus, you will be able to remain within the boundaries where God's love can reach and bless you."

"How do you do that? It all sounds so nice when you say it, but how do I lay my hand in Jesus' hand?"

"Get used to telling Jesus everything. He understands you and loves you. You might say to Him, 'Jesus, I need money badly. I can make a lot of money quickly if I go to that bar and plan a little job with one of my friends. I can also get something to drink there, and I really want a drink. Jesus, take my hand, fill me with Your Holy Spirit. Keep me from falling!'

"If you say that, Jesus will help you. He is not only willing but also able to help you. Ask Him to help you find people who love Him and who are willing to show you how to understand the Bible. Fellowship is so important. Read the Bible much. When you find a text that helps you more than others, write it down, put it in your pocket, and learn it by heart.

"Mike, the most important thing is *trust Jesus*. He will help your faith to grow. In

Hebrews 12 He is called the author and finisher of your faith. I like helping you very much and pray that the Lord will give me wisdom on advising you. Jesus likes to help you even more, and He *really* is able to help."

46

Joe

❧

"I heard your talk today about how to become a child of God by Jesus Christ. It made me anxious to do it. But, lady, you do not know what kind of a guy I am. I have murdered people, and don't ask me how! Let's be honest—I am a lousy guy. No, I am not made of the wood from which you can cut and shape a Christian."

"Joe, there are two ways that we know our sins. The devil accuses us night and day. I don't know if you know the devil. I know him. He speaks very clearly, and he says, 'What you have done is what you are and what you will always be. There is no hope for you.'

"The devil is a liar! The Bible tells us something different. When you bring your sins to Jesus, when you confess your sins, He is faithful and just to forgive you, and He will cleanse you with His blood. You don't understand that? It does not matter. He does it, and it works!

"The Bible also promises that He will put your sins as far away from you as the east is from the west. It is as though He has cast them into the depths of the sea—forgiven and forgotten."

I met Joe again a month later. He looked quite different. The first thing he said was, "I have done it! I was totally miserable! They put me in the hole, which I had feared they would do. I had been in there before for a very long time.

"On my first day in it again, I figured I had nothing to lose, and I said, 'God, if You do exist, take this miserable life of mine in Your hand.' At that very moment something happened. It was as if I was no longer alone. I can't tell you exactly how it was, but I felt happier than ever before. Was it the Lord who came to me? I could suddenly talk to Him. I remembered everything you had said, and I asked myself, *Is what she said true?*

"I slept better that night than I had for weeks, and when I woke up, I felt that happy feeling again. I must say that the weeks I spent in that hole were happy. I knew I was not alone, and to my amazement, I was taken out of the hole after only two weeks.

"Now, Miss ten Boom, I believe it all! How good it is to read the Bible. You had told me that Jesus knocks at the door of your heart, and so I said, 'Come in.' I have told Him more than anyone else all that I have done wrong, and through that I believe there was a clearing up of the dirty mess."

"Joe, you can read in John 3 what took place in your life. In that chapter Jesus tells about what happens when you accept Him. You were born again. Now God is your Father, Joe, and what a Friend you have in Jesus! I'm so glad that the Bible is not fantasy. It is not imagination, not feelings, not philosophy—it is reality! The greatest reality is that Jesus is here on this earth right now, through His Holy Spirit. You are here. I am here. Jesus is here too."

47

So Long!

When you believe the Lord Jesus Christ and you ask Him to come into your heart and into your life, He gives you *His* freedom and a new dimension of living that circumstances cannot destroy.

We can all get to heaven
Without health—
Without wealth—
Without fame—
Without learning—
Without culture—
Without beauty—
Without friends—
Without ten thousands of things.
But we can never get to heaven without
    Christ.

God promises us forgiveness for what we have done, but we need His deliverance from what we *are*. He conquered death at the cross, and He went to heaven. He pleads for us there.

At the same time He is in heaven, He is also with us! I do not understand it at all, but I know it works. I have experienced His presence in the deepest hell that man can create. I have really tested the promises of the Bible, and believe me, you can count on them.

I know that Jesus Christ can live in us— in you and me—through His Holy Spirit. We can talk with Him. We can tell Him everything. You can talk with Him out loud or in your heart—when you are alone, as I was alone in solitary confinement, or in a place crowded with people. The joy is that He hears each word!

In Ravensbrück, after a terrible winter, it was decided that all prisoners my age and older should be killed. One week before this was to happen, I was set free. Later, I learned that it was done only because of a clerical error. In recording our numbers, my number had mistakenly been transferred from the death column to freedom!

A blunder of man, yes. But I knew it was God's way of telling me that I must share— for the rest of my life—what I had learned about Him.

That is why I wanted to write this book for you. I am eighty-five years old now, and I know that the moment is coming when I will have to die. But I am not afraid of death. I belong to Jesus. All of my tomorrows are in His hands.

You know, eternal life does not start when you go to heaven. It starts the moment you reach out to Jesus. That is where it *all* begins. He never turned His back on anyone, and He is waiting for *you!* God bless you.

Corrie ten Boom was imprisoned by the Nazis during World War II for harboring Jews. Upon her release, she began a worldwide ministry of preaching and teaching. *The Hiding Place* is the best-known book about her life.